Legs!

Anna Claybourne

OXFORD
UNIVERSITY PRESS

OXFORD
UNIVERSITY PRESS

Great Clarendon Street, Oxford, OX2 6DP, United Kingdom

Oxford University Press is a department of the University of Oxford. It furthers the University's objective of excellence in research, scholarship, and education by publishing worldwide. Oxford is a registered trade mark of Oxford University Press in the UK and in certain other countries

Text © Anna Claybourne 2016

Inside cover notes written by Catherine Baker

The moral rights of the author have been asserted

First published 2016

British Library Cataloguing in Publication Data

Data available

ISBN: 978-0-19-837075-8

10 9 8 7

Paper used in the production of this book is a natural, recyclable product made from wood grown in sustainable forests. The manufacturing process conforms to the environmental regulations of the country of origin.

Printed in China by Golden Cup

Acknowledgements

Series Editor: Nikki Gamble

The publisher would like to thank the following for permission to reproduce photographs:

Cover: Shutterstock; **P1:** Shutterstock; **P2:** Shutterstock; **P3:** Shutterstock; **P4:** Shutterstock; **p5:** Shutterstock; Goldmund Lukic/Getty Images; Andrew Howe/Getty Images; **p6:** Cyril Ruoso/ Minden Pictures/Getty Images; Keren Su/Getty Images; Shutterstock; Alamy/Tracy Hebden; iStock/redmal; Barrett Hedges/Getty Images; **p7:** Shutterstock; Mustafa Adam/EyeEm/ Getty Images; Alex Hyde/Nature Picture Library; **p8:** Nature Picture Library/ MYN/Piotr Naskrecki; Shutterstock;Marco Uliana/Alamy; Bob Jensen/Alamy; FLPA/Alamy; **p9:** Shutterstock; Natural History Museum, London/Alamy; Bon Appetit/Alamy; **p10-11:** Philippe Psaila/Science Photo Library; **p12:** Shutterstock.

Contents

No Legs

A slug has no legs.

mamba

fins

cod

2 Legs

A robin has 2 legs.

bat

nest

eggs

duck

4 Legs

A panda has 4 legs.

cub

kitten

cat

rat

6 Legs

A bug has 6 legs.

antenna

mantis

8 Legs

A spider has 8 legs.

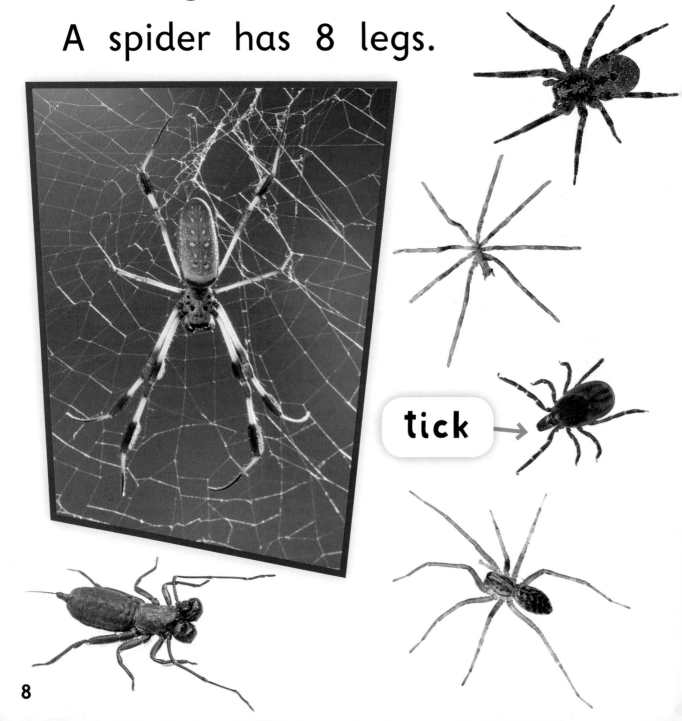

tick

10 Legs

A crab has 10 legs.

antenna

Lots of Legs!

No legs

2 legs

4 legs

6 legs

8 legs

10 legs

Lots of legs!